What we do is about people displaying their fantasies on the outside, trying to break out of the everyday, and look like their dreams.

Ana Matronic, Scissor Sisters

scissor sisters

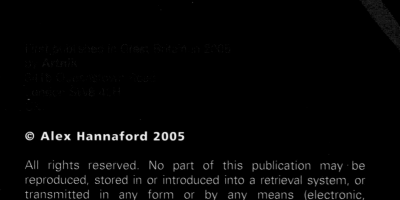

First published in Great Britain in 2005
by Artnik
245b Queenstown Road
London SW8 4CH
UK

ISBN 1–903906–69–5

Design: Supriya Sahai
Pictures: Live Photography
Book Concept: Nicholas Artsrunik
Editor: John McVicar

Printed and bound in Spain by Gráficas Díaz

FOR LIZZIE

This book is an unofficial tribute to Scissor Sisters. The aim was to create something that fans of the band would love to keep – a limited edition book that charts the career, to date, of an act that has fired up the pop charts with some showbiz.

Thanks to Valentina, John and Nicholas at Arthnik – without whom none of these band books would have been possible.

In writing this book I have scoured articles in the following publications:

Scotsman
Coventry Evening Telegraph
Northern Echo
Evening Standard
The Sun
Daily Mirror
Daily Telegraph
Western Daily Press
Chicago Tribune
Sunday Mail
The Guardian
Washington Post
Los Angeles Times
The Observer
The Sunday Times
The Times
The Independent
Sunday Mercury
Western Morning News
The Express
Birmingham Evening Mail
Sunday Mirror
Mail on Sunday

Theage.com
Vh1.com
Inthemix.com
codaagency.com
wikipedia.com
gay.com
nme.com

CONTENTS

Sitting in the little bakery underneath his apartment in a seedy area of Manhattan, Jake Shears drank his coffee while jotting down lyrics for a song that he was writing. The sweet smell of bread baking in the ovens complemented the roasty bitter aroma of the coffee. It was 1999 and Jake was in his last semester at New School University's Eugene Lang College, studying to be a journalist. He claimed that he wanted to be an entertainment reporter but that was the acceptable public face of his secret desire to become a rock star. Hence the lyrics.

He also loved music and harboured a secret ambition to become a rock star. As Aerosmith sang:

'Sing with me, if it's just for today
Maybe tomorrow the good Lord will take you away

Dream on, dream on, dream on,
Dream yourself a dream come true'

But reality bites.

Jake had a look around, took another sip of coffee and remembered he was living in a tiny apartment – just one floor up from a crack den – and was in one of the scariest neighbourhoods in New York. Back then there were few signs that five years on, after selling over one and a half million albums in the UK alone he would be standing on stage, accepting a Grammy award on behalf of his band Scissor Sisters, and could count Bono, Elton John and Kylie Minogue among his friends. As the coffee refills kept coming, Jake looked through the misted window of the bakery onto the street outside. Steam was **billowing** in spurts from the manhole covers in the road and his eyes glazed over.

'I know it's everybody's sin
You got to lose to know
how to win.'

the dream

Jake Shears was born Jason Sellards in Friday Harbour – a little island north of Seattle in Washington State. Once a busy seaport, Friday Harbour's economy is now fuelled by tourism and people flock to see its Orca and Minke Whales, seals and porpoises, while bald eagles circle overhead.

His mum nicknamed him Jake when he was young and the name stuck.

Jake's mother was a larger-than-life Southern woman with a great sense of humour. His dad, by contrast, was rather cranky and conservative.

Jake loved acting and from the age of 10 he was appearing in as many high school plays as he could audition for. He also quickly discovered that, in addition, he had a talent for singing – in falsetto. But Jake was tiring of the small town attitudes of Friday Harbour. It wasn't the greatest place for a teenager – particularly a gay teenager – and its values didn't sit well with him. He his first boyfriend when he was 13 years old, which was seen by puritanical Mormon classmates as real 'pervy'. Their attitude only made him more outrageous. 'What doesn't kill you makes you stronger,' he later boasted. He also likes to quip how quickly he 'went all the way… up, darling. It didn't hurt a bit.'

In his teens he liked to try on girls clothes and wear make-up. Something of an attention-seeker, he would turn up to school in dresses and fishnet stockings.

When he was 15 he donned a wig and sang the Whitney Houston classic 'I Will Always Love You' for a high school show, calling himself 'Whip-me Houston'.

At home he would watch his mum's Jane Fonda Workout video and listen obsessively to Dolly Parton.

Ohh, these camp bitches.

9

"Is it about me being gay?"

Thankfully, it was something his parents would eventually accept.

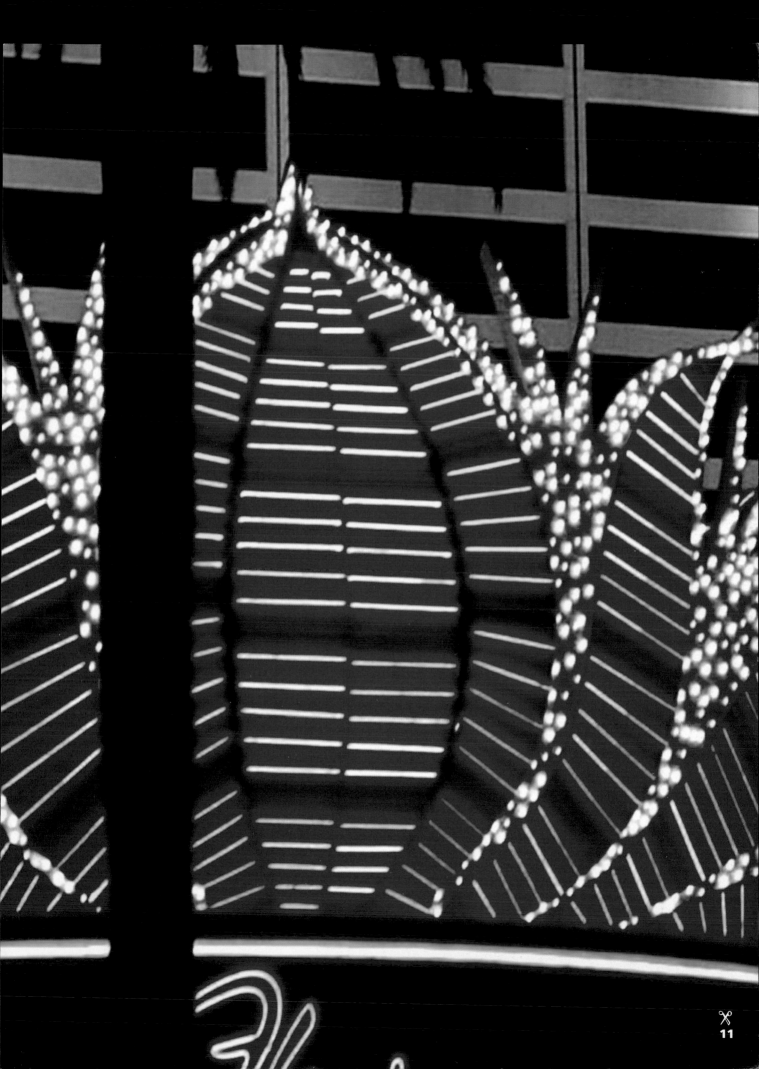

Around the same time he started an electronica band which he called 'My Favourite Band', for which he wrote all the songs, including the hilariously-titled 'I Had Sex With Your Sister'. But he could only play five chords on the guitar and this first crack at making it as a rock 'n' roller floundered because of poor musicianship.

After high school he worked part-time in Bimbo's Bitchin' Burrito Kitchen and a record store called Sub Pop Megamart, but after mooching around Seattle for a year or so Jake decided it was time to head to California to attempt to become a film-maker in Los Angeles. But it wasn't for him.

He hated LA - he had his own dreams but LaLa-Land was too dreamy for words.

In 1999 he travelled to Lexington, Kentucky, to visit a friend of a friend called Scot Hoffman. Hoffman's nickname was Babydaddy and, like Jake, he had also had to deal with growing up gay in a city that wasn't as forward thinking as the huge coastal metropolises of the United States.

Lexington was surrounded by farmland and billed itself as the 'horse capital of the world'. Nobody knows why but, the world over, the horsy set is homophobic.

As a teenager Babydaddy hadn't known a single other gay person.

The two lads hung out for the weekend. 'Jake saw my mom's immaculately clean kitchen and got a bit frightened – as people usually do,' Babydaddy recalled. Over an incredibly a clean kitchen, horror films and video games, Jake and Babydaddy became gay blood brothers, which they are still to this day.

A few months later it was Jake's turn to play host in Seattle where he had taken up residence with a young but seasoned hooker. This was Jake all over. He and Babydaddy bonded further – this time in a much messier kitchen and over the movie *Valley Of The Dolls* which chronicled the glamorous world of backbiting showbiz darlings.

new york

After his uneventful spell in California, Jake headed to New York to study fiction writing and moved into a dodgy apartment in Brooklyn. He tried to make it home as much as possible, but it still looked like a student digs with his unmade bed, clothes strewn over the floor and Roxy Music and Russ Meyer posters stuck to the wall with Blu Tack.

Babydaddy had also moved to the Big Apple and the two renewed their friendship. During his last semester at university Jake managed to get a six-month work experience placement at **Paper** magazine – New York's style bible, covering art and entertainment listings and pop culture for the seriously hip.

'You don't move to New York if you feel accepted in America,'

Babydaddy would say. Here were two people who, as teenagers, had felt estranged from their own home towns because of their sexuality, suddenly feeling like they could finally fit in to society.

Jake started to make some extra cash go-go dancing in an East Village gay bar called I.C. Guys on East Sixth Street, quickly finding he was a bit of a natural under the glare of the spotlight.

'Sometimes I'd leave the place with hundreds of dollars in my back pocket,' he said. 'I was never sleazy, though... I'd pretend that my mom was in the room. It was my way of keeping it clean. And dancing was such an outlet. I loved the attention.'

He was grateful for the work and 'dancing on bars for dollars' as he put it, gave him an incredible amount of confidence after which he felt he could tackle anything the world threw at him. 'Once you've taken your clothes off in front of hundreds of people, things get a lot easier,' he said.
'But the high went, and I got bored. Eventually I was like, "Now I wanna sing".'

15

Jake also loved performance art and his occasional stage shows were becoming more and more over the top. He had invented a character called 'Jason the Amazing Back-Alley Late-Term Abortion' and when he finally took his creation to an East Village bar it went down a storm. A drag queen calling herself 'Mangela Lansbury' pulled Jake on stage in a rubbish bag and he burst out covered in fake blood. 'It looked like there were brains coming out of my head,' Jake told one journalist.

Babydaddy was one delighted spectator that night.

Although college took up a lot of time, Jake and Babydaddy also shared a love of music and would still make time to go to gigs together. They loved the electronica bands that were de rigueur in New York in the late 1990s when the scene was still underground and exciting. But they never twigged that they could ever have a go at making music themselves.

Nevertheless Jake was still writing songs in the studio underneath his apartment, and Babydaddy was still playing guitar and keyboards to keep himself entertained at home. Until one day, Babydaddy mentioned in passing to Jake that he'd been experimenting with a home recording studio. 'Why don't you write some lyrics for some of the stuff I've written,' he recounted. 'I had heard him rap before and knew he had a good sense of humour and was wildly creative. I don't know that I ever knew he was a great singer, but it worked out, and we started writing songs together, which sort of opened me up to discovering that dance music and rock and roll could really be combined in such an interesting way. I discovered Blur, one of those acts

that took dance production and turned it into pop music.

'And I think it was that pop element that really turned me on to dance music in general and discovering artists that sort of blurred the line... from Aphex Twin to, you know, Ace of Base.'

Recalling the latter, he laughed. 'That's one of Jake's sick little pleasures.'

Shears and Babydaddy recorded a couple of singles and started doing shows around New York. Since the city was in the grips of an electroclash fever, making overnight art-world stars out of any two idiots with a broomstick and a steady supply of eye shadow, the pair found people open to bands performing in unconventional ways.

'We had dreams of rock and roll and being a proper band, but the tools that we had to make music sort of overshadowed that in the beginning,' Babydaddy said. 'It was like, "OK, we don't need to haul around a drum kit and do all these things right now, because we can use a computer and get by with whatever we have." It was a time when you could go up on-stage as anything. A lot of the acts that we performed with don't do the full-band thing – they'll bring along samplers and sequencers and do all that stuff. For us it was just always on the horizon, this idea to slowly build, to do this right.'

And when the pair finally collaborated, they knew they had something.

After a couple of months Jake and Babydaddy decided they were ready to take their show on the road. Or at least the clubs on the Lower East Side. Meantime, they went to a screening of Michael Jackson's Captain EO at Disneyland and met an interesting woman called Ana, then later on the Teacup ride they swapped notes on their favourite bands. Jake recalled, 'I really thought she was a freak but when I started singing "Just Another Part of Me" [Michael Jackson] she showed me the best moonwalk I've ever seen.'

It was then that the three realised they shared influences ranging from early nineties Cologne acid-house to *The Muppet Show*; their mutual fate was sealed in the Haunted Mansion with a pair of rusted scissors and bound index fingers. The trio thumbed a ride in the parking lot and headed to Manhattan, where they have been turning it out ever since...

When they told her their band's name – Fibrillating Scissor Sisters – it cracked Ana up. Scissor sisters is a lesbian term for a position in which two women entwine legs and rub each other off. She knew that two gays performing as the Fibrillating Scissor Sisters would, however they played, blow away the audience the the club where she moonlighted as a performance artist.

By day, Ana was Ana Lynch, secretary for a financial law firm but at night she was Ana Matronic, performance artist extraordinaire. She chose the name because...

'I have a deep and abiding love of robots.'

To consecrate her love Ana had her upper right arm and shoulders tattooed with cyborg circuitry and robotic hydraulics. She performed at the Knock Off club where she would do drag queen stuff and way out sketches on lesbians.

Ana is pleased to claim that she comes 'from a long line of wild women'. Her grandmother had joined the legion of girls who, after WW1 had steadfastly refused to settle down into domesticity, preferring to smoke, drink, dance, work and vote. Her only achievement at university was to win a best legs competition.

A generation later, Ana's mother Sherry became a hippy in San Francisco in the late 1960s, after having left Louisiana when President Kennedy was assassinated in Dallas.

During her bohemian period, Sherry met Ana's father Robert and six weeks after they married. Eighteen months later had a daughter, Kate; then another two years on, in 1972, Ana was born. The family went to live lived in Portland, Oregon, known as the City of Roses, just 70 miles from the ocean and one of the most picturesque sections of the coast. However, when she was 3 years old, her father decided he had to come out and left the family home for the bathhouse scene in San Francisco.

Ana and her older sister Kate were raised by their mother Sherry who, having studied religious art in Istanbul, made a living by painting religious icons. A former hippie turned on to a period of art history famed for its conservatism!

The Byzantine Empire which succeeded the Roman Empire was marked by huge domed churches and decorative mosaics, but which left little room for personal expression as far as the artist was concerned. Sherry's inspiration was the Suleymaniye Mosque with its cascading domes dominating the skyline on the Golden Horn's west bank.

Ana inherited her mother's passion for art and later, like the late Freddie Mercury of Queen, she became fascinated with Japanese art, in particular, origami. 'I love the way Japanese art combines the simple with the profound,' she told one journalist.

In Portland, she went through her 'classic-rock phase', so she grew up listening to the big stadia-performers of the 70s and 80s, especially Pink Floyd. She inherited her love of music from her father and listened incessantly to her stereo; she also loved to write songs about 'outsider girls' with weird haircuts. She was a fan of Siouxsie & the Banshees, particularly lead singer Siouxsie Sioux who had courted controversy in the beginning stages of the Banshees by wearing 'bondage' clothes and fetish wear. Unusually for someone her age, she listened to Ornette Coleman – an avant-guard saxophonist from Texas who used electronic accompaniment in his ensembles.

As a child Ana always identified with the wicked queen characters in Disney films – 'the ones that turned into dragons' – and tended to sympathise more with the unconventional outsiders than the goody-too-shoes contingent. Her upbringing fostered free thinking.

'I was raised without boundaries,'

Matronic says. 'I was told I could achieve whatever I wanted with my life, and I was always blessed with an overabundance of love and support.'

When she six, her father told her that he was gay but she was too young to really understand what it meant. They stayed close and, at 13, he took her to New York City for the first time and she fell in love with its charm and excitement in an instant. She recalled later, 'Getting off that plane when I was 13 and seeing Manhattan, I knew I was going to live there one day.' She loved the architecture, the frenetic life of the streets and, most of all, Broadway. Robert loved to watch musicals and he took his daughter to see her first cabaret on Broadway.

A year later her older sister told her that their father had been diagnosed with Aids. He'd had it for some time and his lover took it upon himself to tell the family. Ana, now 14, fully appreciated what it meant and it shattered her world. Robert became painfully thin and their neighbours guessed the cause. There was a huge stigma attached to the disease and the hostility his condition provoked forced them to move to another part of Portland. At school, Ana just said that her father had cancer.

By Christmas 1989, when Ana was 15, her father developed pneumonia and died a couple of days later. In January her beloved grandmother died too. 'That really was the worst year of my life,' she still says.

Robert's funeral was particularly hard, simply because he had died so prematurely; his partner, Don, was there, but after the service Ana and her sister heard no more from him. Nonetheless, after finishing college, in what she believes was a subconscious attempt to get close to her father's spirit, Ana went to San Francisco and immersed herself in the city's burgeoning gay scene. She became one of the few women performers at a drag club called Trannyshack, which billed itself as 'the last stop for bohemian San Francisco'.

One review claimed it was 'the ruler of Tuesday nights in gay clubs… part club night, part tranny burlesque, and all a delightful mess. It's not for the faint of heart.' Ana called performing there 'instant gratification'. She added, 'It was great fun and it really was not your standard Priscilla Queen of the Desert acts.'

Her mother was pretty tolerant of Ana's surreal interests and would occasionally watch her stage act. However, in 1999, Ana decided to move to New York – the city she had fallen in love with as a teenager. Initially she planned to work on a dance project but ended up running a one-night-a-week cabaret event instead. The event was called Knock

Off and took place at the popular club Slipper Room with its Victorian-inspired, jewel-box stage and where bizarre theme nights had names such as 'Dada A-Go-Go' or 'Gore Vidal Sassoon'.

New York Metro described Slipper Room as 'an upstart burlesque house' that had 'sashayed onto the corner of Stanton and Orchard to slap some life into this fratty, grungy stretch … The Slipper Room evokes a pre-Giuliani era of old-fashioned va-va-voom boisterousness crammed into a glittery, sequined halter top of a room with a little stage at the rear for showgirls (and boys) to shake their stuff.'

The Knock Off club night was also a typically over-the-top outlandish venue. A **Village Voice** reporter wrote that it 'served up a racy, multigender revue of kitsch…' He claimed that he was still recovering from one performer, who dressed as a giant vagina,

'…enfolded me with her labia while singing "Lick Me in My Wet Spot" to the tune of "Hit Me With Your Best Shot".'

It was not a place for those of a sensitive disposition.

At Knock Off there was an 'open stage policy' and anyone who wanted to perform, could. 'We had the most ridiculous and stupid performances,' Ana lamented, 'and also stuff that was really beautiful and could be seen as something with a little bit more artistic merit than just a lip sync.'

This was where, on September 21, 2001 (only 12 days after al-Qaeda's attack on the twin towers), Jake and Babydaddy first performed with Ana. She was dressed as a reject from Andy Warhol's cult Factory studio, when she clambered on-stage to welcome the assembled mish-mash of gayly-dressed afficiondos of her club. The night's theme was 'Origami Orgy (Shake your Butoh)' and at around 1am Ana introduced Jake and Babydaddy to the audience.

Jake was dressed in the guise of 'a back-alley abortion'. They played 'Bicycle of the Devil', which according to Babydaddy, 'has a bit of a weird Asian sound to it that we described as Sisters Of Mercy meets Cher... it was a wretched, hilarious, bizarre, gothy techno-y nightmare.'

Jake did a strip while Babydaddy played and Ana contented herself with prancing around leering at his rig and joining in an occasional chorus. She could holler alright. But after they came off stage that night, sweating and still basking in the after-show glory of their decadent performance, Jake and Babydaddy decided something was missing from the Fibrillating Scissor Sisters.

Ana was tough, glamorous, and could sing. She would make a perfect addition to the band – if she agreed. She didn't take much to persuading. Ana wasn't sure that their judgement was correct but she felt that with her as the third Scissor Sister things would definitely fibrillate.

She said later, 'We always wanted to party but our music and shows are as much for hormonal teenagers and housewives with a dancing bug as it is for the downtown party scene.'

...club was the very heart of the new electroclash scene that had boasted acts like Peaches, Chicks on Speed and Fischerspooner. Peaches – born Merrill Nisker – started out as a Canadian folk singer but migrated to her unique brand of sexually provocative electroclash (her early songs included **Diddle My Skittle** and ...).

Her explicit rap fused with electronic dance music landed her a deal first with German label Kitty Yo and later with London's cool XL recordings – home to the White Stripes. Chicks on Speed, meanwhile, were retro disco duo... Melissa Logan from New York, Australian Alex Murray-Leslie, and Kiki Moorse from Germany, and had assembled at Munich's school of art. Fischerspooner were a New York-based performance art two piece who had added **multimedia, fashion and dance** to their electronic musical escapades.

Electroclash was an amalgamation of punk and dance music with the androgynous style of the 1980s thrown in for good measure. It incorporated fashion and visuals drawn from Vivienne Westwood – who almost single-handedly invented punk fashion in the 1970s **bondage gear, safety pins through noses, and lots of chains** – and Andy Warhol's Factory, which in the 1980s mass produced prints, posters, clothes, and even films designed by the artist.

Electroclash emerged almost as a reaction to the post 9/11 mood in New York. Kids in the city felt the war on terror was a war on anything... were tidy-ish in its aftermath. A lot of the large dance clubs

younger generation to **find a reason to celebrate living differently in the city again**

Luxx was the perfect club to house this decadent new genre. It was tucked away on a quiet stretch of Grand Street in Williamsburg – a neighbourhood in northern Brooklyn, close to Manhattan. It wasn't a huge club by any means, but its graffiti-strewn entrance and satin booths gave it a cool, underground feel. It was from here that the new scene would radiate, and Scissor Sisters (they dropped the Fibrillating soon after Ana joined the group) was the perfect name for a band spawned by the snazzy, gay nightlife scene of New York.

Ana felt she was naturally drawn to gay men as friends in a subconscious attempt to feel closer to her father, Robert. 'I guess I'm trying to form a posthumous closeness with my dad,' she admitted. 'This band formed primarily out of the hearts and minds of two gay men, Jake and Babydaddy. And I also consider myself to be a product of the gay community, because my natural father was gay, so half my chromosomes are from a gay man. I also got my start performing in drag clubs in San Francisco. So I think it's a filter through which four-fifths of the band looks through, and it definitely shapes your aesthetic and how you're introduced to things.

However, it has never been our intention or desire to be the standard-bearer for all gay people, everywhere, always.'

Ana's most quoted description of herself is
'a drag queen trapped in a woman's body',
although everyone acknowledges she is as straight as a Roman road. When Jake is questioned by journalists about the name of the group, ('It's what two women would have to do if they wanted their pussies to rub up against each other, like this') after going into graphic clitoral detail about what the act entails, he likes to add deadpan,

'None of us are lesbians, though.'

But while relishing giving an exposition on the roots of the band, he is always keen to stress that in his opinion, music transcends sexuality. 'I don't believe sexuality really matters when it comes to music,' he insists.

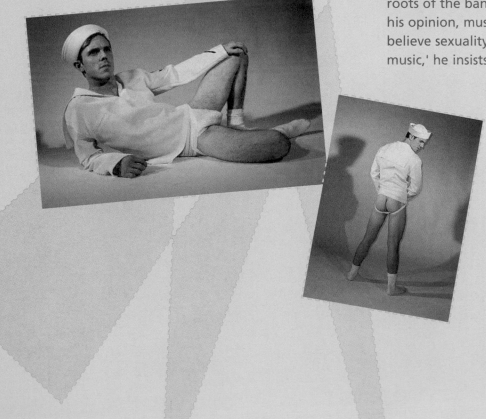

The trio gigged at **Luxx**, then at notorious East Village gay bars such as The Cock, a seedy East Village 'rock and sleaze' hangout. They realised that they would have to expand the musicianship to come out from the electroclash twilight into the lusher pastures of glam disco-rock, to which Babydaddy and Jake were already moving. They took auditions. They tried out rhythm guitarist Derek Gruen, who already knew Jake from his go-go, stripping days.

The BMX-riding guitarist was NY bred and also – like Jake and Babydaddy – gay but what tipped the scales in his favour was he played like Billy Duffy from The Cult. Jake and Babydaddy were fans. In keeping with the lush, glam-rock emerging style of the band, he'd already adopted the stage name Del Marquis – as it comes from a mail order company that sells freaky fetish clothing, the trio saw it as very Scissor Sister-ish.

Del Marquis described joining the band as like 'stepping onto a moving express train'.

drummer Patrick Seacor who because of his Irish ancestry was known as Paddy Boom. Paddy is heterosexual. In a band that is supposedly as camp as a row of tents, Paddy is the envy of most of the players in other groups: 'Any girls looking for some action get passed on to me. I am the envy of every straight guy I know.'

Paddy is always ready to dispel the idea that Sisters are a gay band. 'Having gay members tends to throw people for a loop.' he accepts, 'They tend to think its gay music. My mother did – I had to explain to her that it's not a gay band. It's like I tell her, "Mom, there's gay members, but it doesn't matter. It's about the music and about performance."

'The performance that the band gives is just about putting on a show. Nobody gives a shit whether you go home with a guy or go home with a girl. The sexuality of the band really has nothing to do with what the band is. People want to take shots… but, well, they are really missing the point. Being gay has about as much relevance to the band as being straight does.'

Paddy Boom has been in three bands and admits that playing music has been 'the only steady thing in my whole life'. A year after joining Sisters, he commented in an interview: 'Keith Richards said that being in a band was like being a teenager for ever, and it's true. This last year has been a blast. I love travelling, so it's the ultimate fusion of my passions.' (Before joining Sisters, Paddy spent six months riding a motorbike from New York to Rio de Janeiro.)

-Babydaddy always said to the band, 'Let's make this larger than life.' Del Marquis *jumped* the Scissor Sister express train and found it both larger and faster than anything he'd imagined… Three years later on the Live 8 stage in Hyde Park, his excilerating riffs showed how much he was still enjoying the ride.

Meanwhile, the band continued playing the small venues in New York, then in July 2003 they recruited

Boom's drumming, especially his dexterity on the high hats, walled up the Scissor Sisters' sound, so they were ready for coming out of the small gay club scene to the wider stage. But they knew they could not do that in the USA nor, and more crucially, without some vinyl on the shelves.

Comfortably
Numb

In 2002, Scissor Sisters signed a two single deal with a small New York label called A Touch Of Class, run by New York-based DJs Oliver Stumm and Dominique Clausen, and which released records by Pop Deluxe, Nu Wave Hookers, and Eurochrome, whose single 'Future Spirit' became a club staple with its 1980s-style synthesizer sounds and deep, almost spoke-word vocals (David Bowie style).

Scissor Sisters' first single for the label was Electrobix - a song about the pumping iron cult among gay men ('You gotta pump your body / Ooh you wanna be a honey / You better like to party / You gotta pump that body'). It was released at the end of 2002. But it was the B-side that stormed up the play lists. This was an scintillating cover of the Pink Floyd song 'Comfortably Numb', doubled in speed and with a catchy falsetto from Jake that must have made Bee Gees' Barry Gibb think about joining the castrati. It was an immediate hit in the big dance clubs, too. It had been orchestrated by Babydaddy and Jake before Ana joined the band and she remembered that it was one of the things that confirmed she had joined something special.

'Comfortably Numb was one of four songs that they already had in the can,' she recalled. 'I grew up in the north-west in the States, where everyone has to go through their classic-rock phase, so I grew up listening to Pink Floyd and Jimi Hendrix and the Doors and all those bands. So I already knew the song. Pink Floyd is probably the most sacred of all sacred cows in rock 'n' roll, and when I heard this remake, I thought to myself, "This song has legs a mile long". It's one of those songs that people were either going to love or hate, and that's really, really powerful, because it basically means you're evoking a reaction in everyone. The first time I heard it, I thought that...

if it doesn't make us famous, it'll make us infamous because somebody will shoot us!'

It's just a little pin-prick...
There'll be no more Ahhhhhh!
But you may feel a little sick
Can you stand up, no?
I do believe It's working good
That'll keep you going through
the show...
C'mon it's time to go

'Comfortably Numb' is Pink Floyd's dark peaen to smackhead" and it has a special appeal to those fans who are really into their music. Surprisingly, the band was cool about the Scissor Sisters doing a cover. Babydaddy sent them a copy of it and Pink Floyd's management replied in a brief email "...the writers are very pleased."

'I had this fantasy at the time', Ana remembered with a smile, 'of Roger Walters donning a white three-piece polyester leisure suit and dancing around his living room to our 'Comfortably Numb' and going, "I never thought it could sound like this. Wow!". It was just a little fantasy.'

It came about when Jake was listening to it at his parent's farm in Virginia and he picked up on the way that Walters often underpinned his orchestrations with a disco beat. He suggested to Babydaddy that he bring the beat up front and whip up the tempo.

However, what completely changed the mood of the piece was the surreal video that accompanied it which reworked the drug imagery away from heroin and towards ecstasy.

NME described the effect of the video as 'the aural equivalent of Stephen Hawking wearing glittery hotpants at the local funky nitespot'.

While conceding the shift in drug imagery, Del Marquis was careful to emphasise that the underlying message was

Just-say-No to drugs.

'I thought there's almost a dual meaning, another way to interpret the song. To me it's almost the same thing for a new audience. The original song talks about heroin addiction and losing yourself, and that was also true for dance culture and a different drug… people throwing their lives away.'

Well, he would say that wouldn't he.

The release of 'Comfortably Numb' resulted in a massive amount of airplay, plus a lot of interest from record labels in the UK. Although the band wanted to make on their own material, they were ecstatic at all the attention. They all had the feeling of lift-off.

This UK interest confirmed their gut feel that lifting off would be a lot easier in Europe, especially the UK, than the USA. Middle America is too Springsteen to identify with what the heartland, according to Ana, would call 'a bunch of faggot freaks'. Much of 2003, they spent touring in Europe, using London as their base.

It was difficult to pigeon-hole the Scissor Sisters. While they could initially be grouped together with the electroclash scene and they had come from quite a niche, performance art scene in New York, there was something about their music that transcended both. The songs the trio were starting to write were incredibly catchy for starters.

These were songs that would appeal to a much wider audience. Call it pop if you will, but it certainly wasn't bubble-gum. They had the glitzy stage presence and the songs were difficult to get out of your head.

Here was a band that could potentially be around for a long time... if they played their cards right - which they were.

And their trump card was undoubtedly the music, which Babydaddy and Jake treated with the kind of TLC that most people reserve for their children... in fact, their songs are their children. They may have returned to the passé craft of traditional pop songwriting but they do it with a reverence for melody and meticulous attention to the refinement of lyrics. It makes for easy listening with a subversive Scissor edge. Babydaddy once said, 'Someone described our music as a Trojan Horse – it's the idea that we're presenting something in a very whoesome package, but deep down we're a lot more subversive than everyone realises.'

Marquis told – of all people – a reporter on Moscow's **St. Petersburg Times** in August 2004, 'There are no really good pop bands right now in music, like people who write well-crafted songs, intelligible lyrics, somewhat challenging but still very universal, which can be played on radio or in a dance club.'

"If you're pop now, you're a figurehead, and there's a machine behind you creating everything that you are, or you are an angry rocker. Yet there's just so much more in-between.

And I think that 70s' and 80s' bands wrote amazing pop singles. They designed their own image, everything that you associate with them came from the band. And I think we're harking back to that a little bit. We're not afraid of writing a pop tune, but we're in control of all that.'

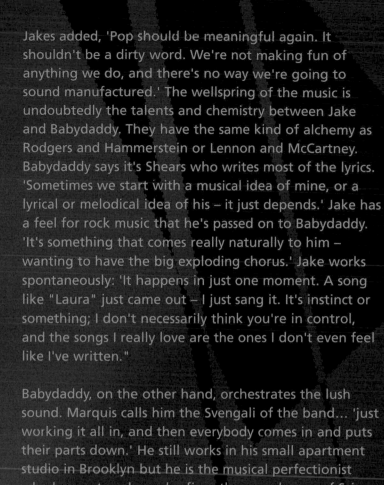

Jakes added, 'Pop should be meaningful again. It shouldn't be a dirty word. We're not making fun of anything we do, and there's no way we're going to sound manufactured.' The wellspring of the music is undoubtedly the talents and chemistry between Jake and Babydaddy. They have the same kind of alchemy as Rodgers and Hammerstein or Lennon and McCartney. Babydaddy says it's Shears who writes most of the lyrics. 'Sometimes we start with a musical idea of mine, or a lyrical or melodical idea of his – it just depends.' Jake has a feel for rock music that he's passed on to Babydaddy. 'It's something that comes really naturally to him – wanting to have the big exploding chorus.' Jake works spontaneously: 'It happens in just one moment. A song like "Laura" just came out – I just sang it. It's instinct or something; I don't necessarily think you're in control, and the songs I really love are the ones I don't even feel like I've written."

Babydaddy, on the other hand, orchestrates the lush sound. Marquis calls him the Svengali of the band... 'just working it all in, and then everybody comes in and puts their parts down.' He still works in his small apartment studio in Brooklyn but he is the musical perfectionist who hones, tweaks and refines the soundscape of Scissor Sisters. He described the eponymous-named album as 'primitively made... We turned sounds that were imperfectly recorded on cheap equipment into something unique. I want to keep doing it that way – I have a fear of coming into money for production. I think money ruins artists. I am a huge fan of Tim Burton, but the second he got big budgets, he ceased being interesting to me.'

'There's something about the struggle that gives art its own life.'

Marquis summarised each of the groups' contribution: 'We are all very different from each other but on stage there is the common purpose, so I think the ingredients are the accident of everybody meeting each other. We all have our own ideas of what we want to be and do onstage and it comes together really well. Jake would definitely be the ringleader, Scissor Sisters is his baby, a musical idea born out of his head.

'Ana brings the theatre and without her many shows would have fallen apart in a matter of seconds. Babydaddy is the Svengali, the Mick Fleetwood character, silent but very powerful, all knowing. Paddy is our good time guy; he never fails to have fun. I am a little bit of a rockers' guitar player, I bring the cock-rock to the Scissor Sisters.'

No wonder The **Village Voice** lauded Scissor Sisters as 'a rock unit who aren't afraid to play disco'.

Complimenting the sound is the showmanship, the videos, the stage sets, the clothes, the histrionics. Jake, of course, is the driving force behind much of that. In January 2005, he told the **Toronto Sun,** 'It all started with the stripping, I did it for, like, a year and a half and then once I started making music, one sort of bled into the other.

'I was singing on stage and still taking off my clothes and wanting tips and realizing that it wasn't necessarily appropriate anymore. I just said, "It was now time to sing and put my pants back on." (Not that the pants don't slip down regularly.) I don't like watching myself perform on tape.

When I do, I'm shocked! I'm very, very loose, to put it mildly...'

'But we're just trying to keep a tradition alive,' Jake emphasises, 'I was just in the Rock and Roll Hall of Fame in Cleveland. Walking through all the wardrobe exhibits, it really spoke to me and made me excited and totally reassured me that what we're doing is part of a long-standing tradition.

𝔇ressing up and wearing crazy stuff and going for it and putting on a show – that's what rock 'n' roll is all about and what it's always been about.

'And I think that somewhere in the past 10 or 12 years, that's gotten lost a little bit, it's gotten a bit more casual, pedestrian. A lot of the time the person on stage looks no different than the person standing next to you in the audience. I think there should be an element of putting on a show, of dressing up and becoming larger than life.'

Jake notes that Elton John and Elvis were the ultimate showmen… 'There's a lot of talk about how outrageous we are and, y'know, how we wear *crrraaazy* clothes and I think it's a little silly. Rock 'n' roll has always been over the top: wearing kooky clothes, putting on a show, putting on the sequins.

the top: wearing crazy clothes, putting on a show, putting on the sequins.

'We're just carrying on a rock 'n' roll tradition.'

Their videos and stage sets are characterised by the same 'larger than life' effect: the bold colours, intricate design, bizarre props (hookers' neon signs), cross-dressing (Babydaddy's suspenders and feather boas). Marquis says of this, 'I certainly know that a lot of times you don't get to see a really visually stunning show from most bands, unless you're going to see Madonna at the 'Girlie Show' tour. Most bands don't really put in the effort, I think. This last tour, we really worked with the money that we were given to do a show that was really interesting visually and that's important to us.'

He notes that when they do covers of other bands, 'You do it out of respect for the band first and then try to make it your own, otherwise you're just playing it. You have to come up with something new.'

This is exactly what the Sisters did in bringing Halloween to England in October 2004, asking fans coming to their Brixton Academy concert to glam up for the evening, which they did in a mix of standard horror costumes and more imaginative original outfits. Scissor Sisters did their part dressing up as characters from their favorite film, *The Rocky Horror Picture Show*. Jake described the happening, **'It was magical, I'm telling you and went beyond my expectations.** They don't dress up for Halloween over there – they don't even really celebrate it – but 5,000 people showed up decked out and it was so much fun.'

Talking with American University's **The Eagle** in July 2004, Del Marquis said of their use of dance on stage, 'I think that should always be there in rock and pop music, but I think somewhere along the way people lost

the idea that you can incorporate rhythm and dance into straight forward rock songs. That never really got lost on people in the U.K.'

Ana added, 'It's kind of annoying, I think that there's been a perception in recent years that if you dress up and put on a show, your music isn't as honest as somebody who wears their T-shirt and jeans and looks at their feet. We would definitely like to challenge that notion.'

Christopher Hickman of **Flak** wrote after the release of *Scissor Sisters*: 'Before grunge's stranglehold choked the joy out of rock and hip-hop's self-serving moneymakers began rapping exclusively about their bank accounts, it used to go without saying that this is the way popular music is supposed to be: madcap stories from wildly charismatic people who are doing what they do because they love it – entertainers who know that the onus is on them to be entertaining.

'Whether you like the Scissor Sisters or not, their ardent attention to melody, song structure and fun, just fun, is transparent on their debut. It's obvious how much they care when listening to mega-disco jams like "Take Your Mama" and "Tits on the Radio," the Barry Gibb-inspired falsetto on their dance revision of Pink Floyd's "Comfortably Numb," and even "Filthy/Gorgeous," the one song on the album that sounds distinctly like electroclash and gives listeners a clue to the band's roots in Larry Tee's bedroom-DJ Williamsburg scene. Scissor Sisters are not so easily contained. Frontman Jake Shears, multi-instrumentalist Babydaddy, singer Ana Matronic, guitarist Del Marquis and drummer Paddy Boom have absorbed some 30 years of disparate styles and have trusted their instincts.

Their songs, as a result, brim with soul and panache.'

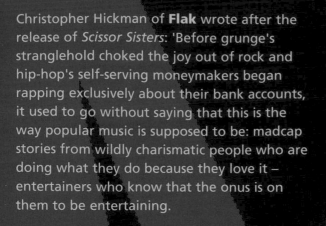

At the Toronto's The Guvernment in January 2005, Jake and Ana also worked another of the Scissor's trademarks, some jokey obscenity. She told the screaming and steaming crowd that she hoped the men would be 'eating pussy' while they listened to 'Rock my Spot'; before he launched into it, our fag-tastic frontman quipped, 'I ain't gonna eat it, but don't let me stop y'aaaallllll.'

Scissor Sisters look the way their music sounds.

The band sings, but more than that - it performs.

2004
scissor sisters cut it

Their first album, Scissor Sisters, was released in the UK in February 2004 and included their trailblazing 'Comfortably Numb'. It sold 1,500,000 by the end of year and was the UK's biggest selling album in 2004. It wasn't released until August in the USA, where it only did 150,000. The sales vindicated the shift to touring in the UK and what Ana used to tell audiences: 'I say again and again and again, let's not forget that America was founded by the Puritans and all the pagans stayed over in Britain.' Well, present company excepted, especially the ones who perform saucy '70s-vibe-style pop songs and like to dress as if they were attending a convention for pimps and hookers.

Dedicated to the album format, the band – especially Babydaddy and Jake – for months over the track order, sonic nuances and overall length. Inspired by the classic rock albums of thirty years ago, the goal was, according to Babydaddy, '...to create a perfect pop rock album that would pick you up at the beginning, take you on a journey in the middle, and set you right back down in the same place at the end.

Every step we took, we looked at history... I think we as a culture are going to need entire albums in addition to just "songs".

I have a great love for the pop song – Lord knows we all have a short attention span at times. Yet there are days when you want to watch a sitcom and other days when you want to see a film. The song and the album are clearly two different circumstances. When I look back on my childhood, my most profound experiences were sitting in my room listening to entire records. That, to me, is a pensive, personal moment when an artist speaks to me and relates an entire story, not just a little anecdote.'

Ana tells a similar story, 'We gave ourselves the time to really work on the music, and let it evolve and let ourselves evolve as far as production, musicianship and singing and songwriting went. I think that time really served us well. It was in that time that songs like "Mary" and "Lovers in the Backseat" came out, which I think are a lot more fleshed out and realised than some of the earlier stuff.

'We really wanted every song to be as good as it possibly could be,' she continues. 'In the '60s and '70s, artists really worked on albums, and there was something conceptual behind what they were doing: an album was a full piece.

It wasn't ever about singles and filling everything up. It wasn't ever about making a number-one song.

It was about making a good, consistent-sounding, quality record, and that's what we wanted to do. We're all kids from the mid to late '70s and the first music we all collectively listened to and responded to were bands like the Beatles, bands that didn't just make songs, they made albums. For the most part, music now seems so singles-driven and so sales-driven, and it's sad to me that so much artistry has seemingly fallen by the wayside. It's pretty tragic.'

Babydaddy pointed out at the time, 'We've fought like hell just to get this album out here with all the songs intact. The decision was made by us not to put the album in Wal-Mart, and not to make a clean version. We did have to slap a parental warning sticker on the disc, which is completely absurd. I think a kid listening to Eminem is getting a much more negative message that what we've been putting forward.

We've only got one 'shit' and a few 'tits'!

The Scissor Sisters album, with its kitsch, technicolour flamboyance, skillful songwriting, sparkling virtuosity, infectious energy and simply great songs, made the group. From the hammering piano riff and Dexy's Midnight Runners' bounce of 'Laura' and the Elton-pop of 'Take Your Mother Out', to the throbbing disco and falsetto vocals of 'Comfortably Numb' and the melodramatic 'Return to Oz', the album became a self-indulgent, decadent soundtrack for a night on the tiles.

The final track, 'Return of Oz', was written by Jake and is a stirring finale to a superb album. Jake's lyrics chronicle a close friend's addiction to the drug, but told in the imagery of the *Wizard Of Oz* .

Hillbilly Crack, as crystal meth was otherwise known, was fast becoming a major issue in U.S cities. Users had rotting, brittle teeth and the drug could be manufactured easily in discreet little homemade labs from household chemicals. The resulting powder could be smoked, injected or snorted.

*To return to Oz, we fled the
world with smiles and
clenching jaws*

*Please help me friend from
coming down*

*I've lost my place and now
it can't be found*

It is probably the most powerful song Jake has ever written and it alone was an example of how Scissor Sisters were not just another pop act.

'To me,' Babydaddy says, 'it's a song about San Francisco and to a lot of others it's about New York but it can be about anywhere. I wouldn't say that it was one specific incident, but I think everyone in the band and in our group of friends has been touched in some way by the problems it's talking about.

'It is talking about the problems of the homogenisation of the gay community and people losing themselves in self-deprecation, then losing themselves in an escape that's not a positive escape. It's a retracting from reality.

'Like the early works of Bowie, Morrissey or the Pet Shop Boys, Scissor Sisters' music often pitches itself against the claustrophobia of modern life,' **The Observer** wrote, 'and tries to make sense of paranoia and hysteria in supposedly enlightened times.'

The cover art of *Scissor Sisters* featured a girl in a virginal white dress in an almost *Alice Through the Looking Glass*-style world. You could only see the back of her as she was about to walk from a forest through a large circle into the hustle and bustle of New York City. On the bottom right hand corner of the record sleeve was a parental advisory 'explicit content' warning.

The artwork was by a Brighton-based English illustrator who went by the name of 'Spookytim'. He had created the picture using a mixture of traditional paper based techniques alongside digital trickery and regular photography.

Guardian music journalist Paul Lester called it 'the first post-electroclash masterpiece: an album that recalls the hits of Elton John, the Bee Gees and late-1970s disco queen Sylvester'.

Scissor Sisters' London agency, Coda, purple-prosed band at the time of the album: 'Think grass-roots psychedelica infused with explosive disco arena anthems, accordions swaying over tight hip-hop loops, falsetto loveliness clashing with dirty post-punk fuzz bass, and corn-poke country rave-ups running riot over traditional four-to-the-floor dance club thrust. All of this unified by meticulous songcraft, meaty hooks, lyrical irreverence and innovation combined with unbridled honesty and a strong dose of unabashed, hands-in-the air fun.

A London promoter tagged them as "Wham-meets-Ween," which suits them just fine.'

Wham, bam, thank you Ma'am, as Jake might say.

If jazz is an art form, so is rock 'n' roll. And in that case Scissor Sisters are artists. And one thing real artists do is work hard...

Jake remembers, 'Our debut album *Scissor Sisters* came out in February and entered the charts at number 11. We were happy, but the record could still have been dead in the water. A week later, we played an energetic, somewhat wonky show at the Scala in London and at a party afterwards, the editor of a British music magazine pulled me aside and said: "You've got a great band, but you're going to have to get tighter." I took it to heart, and if anything was going to make us tighter, it would be touring our brains out.'

After the Scala gig, **The Times** described the performance as

'a sweaty night out for poseurs, groups of gay men and women with trendy handbags'.

Jake was ecstatic. It reminded him of all the kids at school who had teased him, called him a 'faggot' and made his life hell, yet now he had achieved more in just a few years than most of them would in a lifetime. 'The greatest pop music is always an act of revenge,' he said. 'It's pivotal to fame and anyone who says it isn't is lying. It's giving those kids the middle finger.'

He remembered the music editor's advice: 'We toured, and played and sang and danced until we could barely get out of our bunks. Some of it was a blast, other parts were miserable. I got an eye infection and had to wear an eye patch on stage. I thought I'd make the most of it and adopt a more sinister persona for three or four performances.'

'We loved playing at the Louisiana in Bristol. The Social in Nottingham was a blast. Supporting Duran Duran on tour was wild. Wembley was the first really big crowd we had ever played for. I think we were all pretty nervous that first night. But the moment we were on stage, I realised how much I love a huge audience.

The trick, I guess, is to make the venue feel small – you have to exaggerate all your moves.

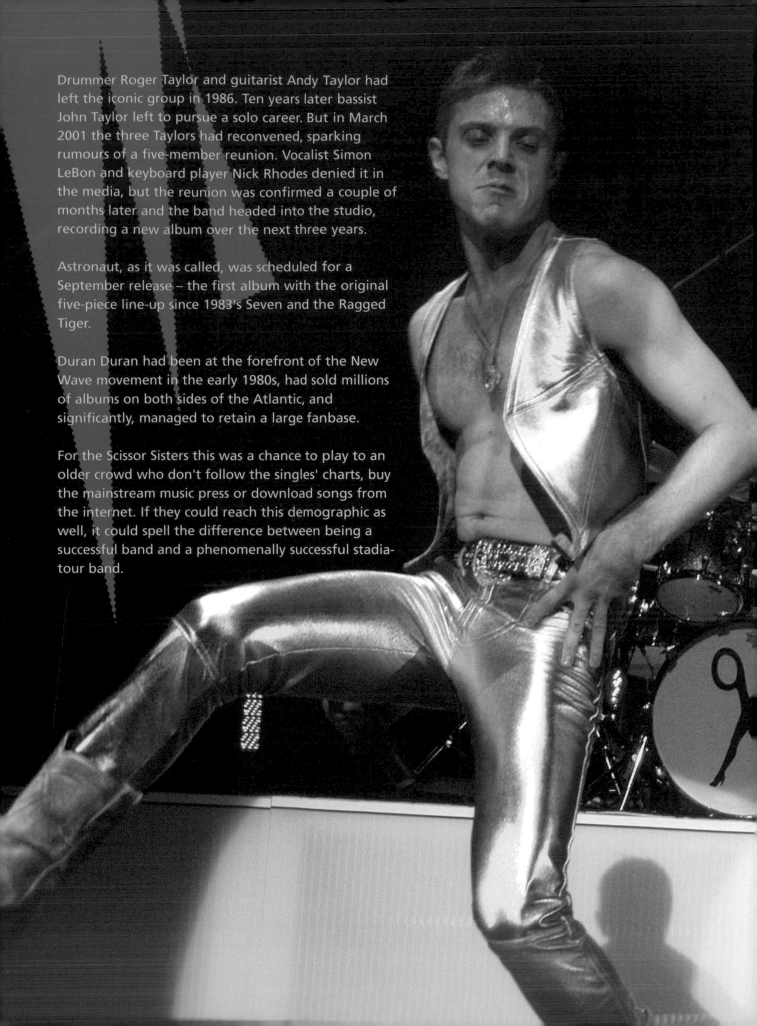

Drummer Roger Taylor and guitarist Andy Taylor had left the iconic group in 1986. Ten years later bassist John Taylor left to pursue a solo career. But in March 2001 the three Taylors had reconvened, sparking rumours of a five-member reunion. Vocalist Simon LeBon and keyboard player Nick Rhodes denied it in the media, but the reunion was confirmed a couple of months later and the band headed into the studio, recording a new album over the next three years.

Astronaut, as it was called, was scheduled for a September release – the first album with the original five-piece line-up since 1983's Seven and the Ragged Tiger.

Duran Duran had been at the forefront of the New Wave movement in the early 1980s, had sold millions of albums on both sides of the Atlantic, and significantly, managed to retain a large fanbase.

For the Scissor Sisters this was a chance to play to an older crowd who don't follow the singles' charts, buy the mainstream music press or download songs from the internet. If they could reach this demographic as well, it could spell the difference between being a successful band and a phenomenally successful stadia-tour band.

The Duran Duran support slot included four nights at Wembley Arena – the biggest audience Scissor Sisters had ever played to. The fans whooped and stomped… Scissors had cut it.

Jake recalled the next big step up: 'It was around this time that we got a phone call from Elton John's people, wondering if we'd like to open for him in June. I had been wondering for months what the hell he would think of us. But it wasn't until we played at a party for **Attitude** magazine that we managed to meet. A friend told me he was in the audience. I could have strangled him – the last thing you want to know is that your heroes are watching you. But I couldn't help but notice George Michael strolling past before we went on stage.

'Elton sat at the back and whenever we finished a song, instead of clapping, he would hold his hand out, palm facing the stage. I took this as a sign of approval. Afterwards, he and George and their crew came back to the dressing room.

'Talking to Elton, I felt like I was suddenly speaking with a pastor, priest or rabbi of rock 'n' roll. I told him how insane everything had been. He replied,

"Welcome to showbusiness!"

squeezing both my cheeks with each hand.'

Elton told Jake that he had been listening to Scissor Sisters' record whilst recording his latest album and that he'd bought 50 copies to hand out to his friends. In actual fact, rumour had it that he listened to *Scissor Sisters* every morning to start his day

It was an honour Jake didn't think he could ever top. Until, a few days later, he received a call from Elton John's office asking whether the band would open for him at his concert in June.

Jake remembers it like one recalls snatches of a dream on wakening: 'After supporting Elton on tour, the summer festivals went swimmingly; indeed in Portugal we played in a typhoon with people slinging mud at the stage. But it was so exhausting – one time I passed out on the cold, bare floor in front of the British Airways counter at Heathrow for three hours.'

One Elton concert took place at Hop Farm Country Park in Kent on Sunday June 20th. Set amongst the world's largest collection of Victorian Oast houses, it was once a working farm and has now become one of the South East's most popular attractions.

During their set, Jake accidentally did his usual impromptu strip show for 20,000 onlookers.

'My trousers burst open and it just fell out,' he said. 'So I walked over to my drum tech and had him stick a big piece of gaffer tape on my crotch.'

Despite this technical hitch, the audience loved the show... so it seemed did Elton as he sang and played piano for two and a half hours.

By this point Scissor Sisters had also become something of a hit in the fashion world as well, courting mentions in the style press on both sides of the Atlantic. Jake was being decked out by designers like Swedish-born Martin Andersson, yet he still claimed he wasn't stylish. 'I don't know whether people expect us to dress like this offstage,' he told **Designer** magazine.

'I don't know whether they expect us to be walking down the road in a purple suede cat suit, but it's just not going to happen.

'I need those things on stage because it brings out and magnifies that part of your personality ... I can't think of anything more boring than fashion though.'

Someone once described Jake's own un-dress sense as '**pube**scent'.

Another of Scissors 2004's breakthroughs was the invitation to star at Glastonbury. The UK festival season kicked off with that Festival at the end of June. Glastonbury has been run by farmer Michael Eavis since 1970 and is the best of all the UK summer festivals.

Jake, Ana, Babydaddy, Del and Paddy had heard it was more of an event than a regular music festival and were told to spend as much time as they could there, soaking up the weirdness of it all. So it was time to dig out the old sleeping bags in preparation for three nights of restless and uncomfortable sleep in between zoning out in the healing field and playing live on stage.

'I don't know if I've ever felt as much energy coming off a crowd as I did during our second set in the dance tent,' Jake said after the festival.

'I've never seen such madness — people off their tits, jamming out to Motown and Aretha.'

It wasn't a life-changing event for the Scissor Sisters but they were moved by what they experienced. The fans seemed to be genuinely rejoicing in the creativity of the music and using it to expand their own consciousness. British politician Tony Benn said back in 2003: 'Glastonbury is a fantastic event. So many young people in a community which is self-governing and tolerant. It confirms my belief that despite everything, humanity really does want to get on with itself.'

Jake confessed, 'When things get bitchy, I think of playing Glastonbury.'

'Another antidote to the bad times is remembering Ana on a plane after a show in Germany. The turbulence was terrible and we were bouncing and dipping all over the damn place. Ana was just sitting in her chair repeating the word "bathtub"' over and over again to herself. She says she read somewhere that you're more likely to die in the bath than on an aeroplane.'

Scissor Sisters gigged all of the UK's major music venues – from Sheffield University to Nottingham Rock City and the Glasgow Barrowland, Jake and Ana would bounce around the stage still visibly excited, like it was still a novelty. But it was something they were going to have to get used to.

The banter onstage between the pair was infectious – ranging from what one reviewer called 'amusingly snarky observations,' to the crudest sexual repartee.

Glasgow was a fantastic venue to play. It only held 1900 people and had been awarded Best Venue in Great Britain in a Radio One poll of over sixty bands.

After Glasgow's Barrowland show Jake said that they were the best crowd ever. 'And we've been around the world playing. They are fantastic. It's such an incredible atmosphere. The Barrowland gig was just so intense and the crowd were very responsive.'

After the show, though, the tour bus broke down leaving the band stranded until a replacement arrived. When their ride finally materialised, the five-piece were tired and irritable. 'Things do get stressed and there is pressure,' Jake would later say.

'It is tough sometimes and you have to be a bitch. But I try and be as nice a bitch as possible.'

Still, being in such close proximity for such long periods of time meant it was inevitable there would be the occasional arguments or tension. 'We drive each other up the wall sometimes,' Jake said. 'I, for one, can be controlling, stubborn and difficult. And that could be said for everybody except Paddy, who carries the least burdensome emotional baggage.'

Scissor Sisters had truly arrived and the five members were relishing every moment. They seemed to gel with everyone who was working with them – from PRs to record company executives to roadies. It was like one big extended family, which made life on the road bearable, particularly as by now they'd graduated to a state of the art tour bus. August was a busy month.

The band flew to Russia for an open-air gig at Moscow's Hermitage Gardens on the 14th. The **St Petersburg Times** ran a piece claiming that, while Russia may still be seen as a haven for burnt-out Western rockers, the arrival of Scissor Sisters was a step in the right direction.

'Although this witty, eccentric band draws from pop music of the late 1970s and early 1980s,' the journalist wrote, 'with David Bowie, Elton John, Blondie, Roxy Music and many others resonating in its instantly catchy songs, it is not a retro affair –

it is fresh and infectious.'

By the 21st they were back in UK for the V festival which took place in both Essex and Staffordshire over the same weekend. Like the Reading festival in Reading and Leeds, bands scheduled to play Essex on the Saturday would head up to Staffordshire on the Sunday and vice versa.

It was a mad dash up north on the Sunday morning – particularly if you were nursing a hangover after your performance. The V festival had been going since 1996 and back then it was the only event of its kind to be staged at two sites over the same weekend where the artists swap venues overnight.

For their show that day in the summer heat, Scissor Sisters won a coveted 'gig of the year' award in a poll of 4,000 Virgin Radio listeners. In second and third place was the Red Hot Chili Peppers' Hyde Park performance and Keane's V Festival appearance.

A month later Jake, Ana, Babydaddy, Del and Paddy were given some more incredible news: their debut album had almost topped one million sales.

Back in the UK, the media attention was A-list celeb with the tabloids covering their every move. The album had been universally praised. Everywhere that was, except Malaysia. The country's **New Straits Times** claimed 'Their much-ballyhooed self-titled debut is for the most part an uneven affair' and 'the campy spirit of the proceedings and the defiantly gay references get a tad tiresome in no time', but even it concluded: 'if you're in the right mood, this could be good fun'.

The touring had seemed relentless but they knew that the first couple of years were vital if they were going to break the back of the country they came from. They were exhausted but excited at the prospect and settled into a life which seemed to revolve around heading to and fro across the Atlantic.

But it was taking its toll, and Jake was becoming frustrated at playing the same set each night. He knew that if they were going to top their debut record they would need a proper break.

They had gigs, interviews and appearances booked up to February 2005 and by that time Jake knew they would have to have a rest and get back into the studio.

'Or else... someone will quit,' Babydaddy said.

Another of Babydaddy's numbers is to be the band's pressure gauge.

Born in the USA

The Scissor Sisters had larged it in the UK, but they were all Americans… And America was a far bigger market! They had to try, especially with Universal breathing down their necks. A journalist for Seatle's **Stranger** magazine and a friend of Jake's wrote of their ambition: 'Take a band named after a lesbian sex act, with three gay members, and hidden queer themes in nearly all of their songs, and try to sell them to homophobic Middle America... and you have a surefire all-American flop.' Scissor Sisters gave it their best Universal-assisted shot.

Following a performance on *Saturday Night Live* – the popular comedy sketch show – they did get some hate mail. But it was almost expected. 'America is often at times not a hugely accepting place, it's a puritanical place,' Babydaddy told one reporter. 'We're open about who we are, and all it gets us is hate mail from people calling us "faggots" and any derogatory name you can think of.'

Nevertheless, the positive fanmail far outweighed the negative, so even Middle America was coming round. The press in the UK watched with interest as the band attempted to woo their home crowd. One reporter even wrote that 'infiltrating Middle America with their neon pop campery' was a 'noble ambition'.

With the gay marriage issue splitting America down the middle, Jake thought he could use his new-found fame as a pedestal to add his voice to the debate. 'George Bush is using this as a smokescreen for everything, which is just sick,' he stated.

When we release the record in America, it's going to get political.

'The entertainment industry is so silent… mostly everybody keeps quiet about anything that's going to rock their boat… the possibilities there are now for gay relationships are endless.'

Babydaddy may think he is – and may actually be – a lot smarter than Bob Geldof, but gay marriage can never equate with an African child dying of 'extreme poverty' every three seconds. George Bush shifted ground on debt relief for Africa but, predictably, was not infiltrated one iota by neon pop campery.

Nonetheless, Universal did release Scissor Sisters in the USA some six months after the UK launch. US labels often use the UK as a testing ground for indie bands but success in England guarantees nothing in the States. Tricia Romano, a columnist on the **Village Voice** told the UK's **Guardian** 'thanks to the morons in the middle of the country, the music scene stinks. With the presidential election… the country is evenly split. Do you expect these people to make sensible decisions about music? If Scissor Sisters did succeed, they'd be in bad company.'

Still, the band was determined. 'Besides,' Jake said, if anybody thinks Will Young and I are the only gay singers working today, they're crazy.' Perhaps the U.S was ripe for a bit of controversy.

Jake believed the band stood for bringing people together, regardless of their political beliefs, religion or sexual orientation. He came from a right wing, Christian family. 'I can still have fun with a Republican,' he said. 'I'm really interested in unifying people, and if that means Republican housewives coming to the shows, that gets me excited.' The band hoped that, regardless of politics or religion, people could listen to their music and enjoy it.

Marquis said that if the band got airplay on what he termed 'mum and dad radio' in the States, it would represent a revolution of sorts.

A bit of subversiveness in middle America

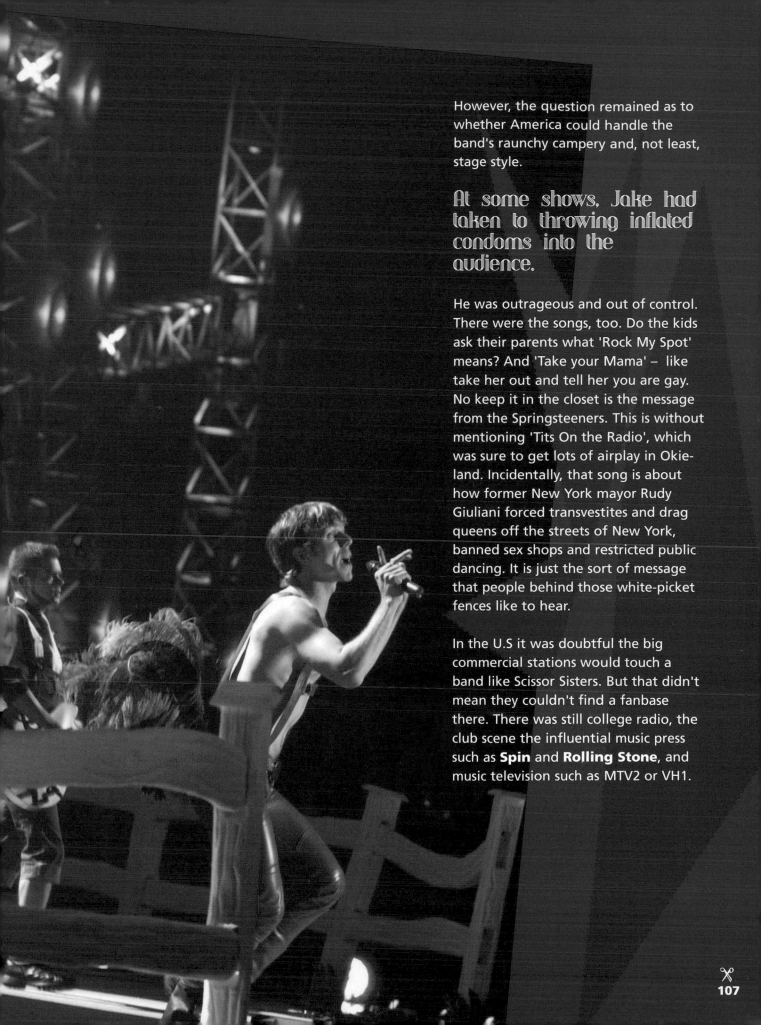

However, the question remained as to whether America could handle the band's raunchy campery and, not least, stage style.

At some shows, Jake had taken to throwing inflated condoms into the audience.

He was outrageous and out of control. There were the songs, too. Do the kids ask their parents what 'Rock My Spot' means? And 'Take your Mama' – like take her out and tell her you are gay. No keep it in the closet is the message from the Springsteeners. This is without mentioning 'Tits On the Radio', which was sure to get lots of airplay in Okie-land. Incidentally, that song is about how former New York mayor Rudy Giuliani forced transvestites and drag queens off the streets of New York, banned sex shops and restricted public dancing. It is just the sort of message that people behind those white-picket fences like to hear.

In the U.S it was doubtful the big commercial stations would touch a band like Scissor Sisters. But that didn't mean they couldn't find a fanbase there. There was still college radio, the club scene the influential music press such as **Spin** and **Rolling Stone**, and music television such as MTV2 or VH1.

Bizarrely, in August 2004, the band managed to secure two slots on the morning television chat show *Live With Regis and Kelly*. This was the UK equivalent of an appearance on ITV's *This Morning*; *Regis and Kelly* was popular with 'stay-at-home-mums' and grandparents. Jake thought the whole episode was hilarious. He wore a loud shirt and hammed it up for the cameras.

Jake recalled, 'Kelly Ripa loved us, after the first time we played, she gave me a hug and whispered in my ear, "I just want you to know that this is my favourite music performance we've ever had." It was amazing. Regis was really excited that we were there. I made a dirty joke. Regis didn't even get it, and it made it on the air.'

'He asked, "What is a Scissor Sister?"

And I was like, "I can't really say what it is on this show," but I took his hand and went like this (Jake spread his third and fourth fingers on both hands and rubbed them together in an entwined position) and Kelly and Regis were like, "Oh. My. God."

'Then Regis was like, "You guys are called Scissor Sisters, but I only see one lady up here!" I replied, "Yeah! You'd be surprised!" That cracked me up.'

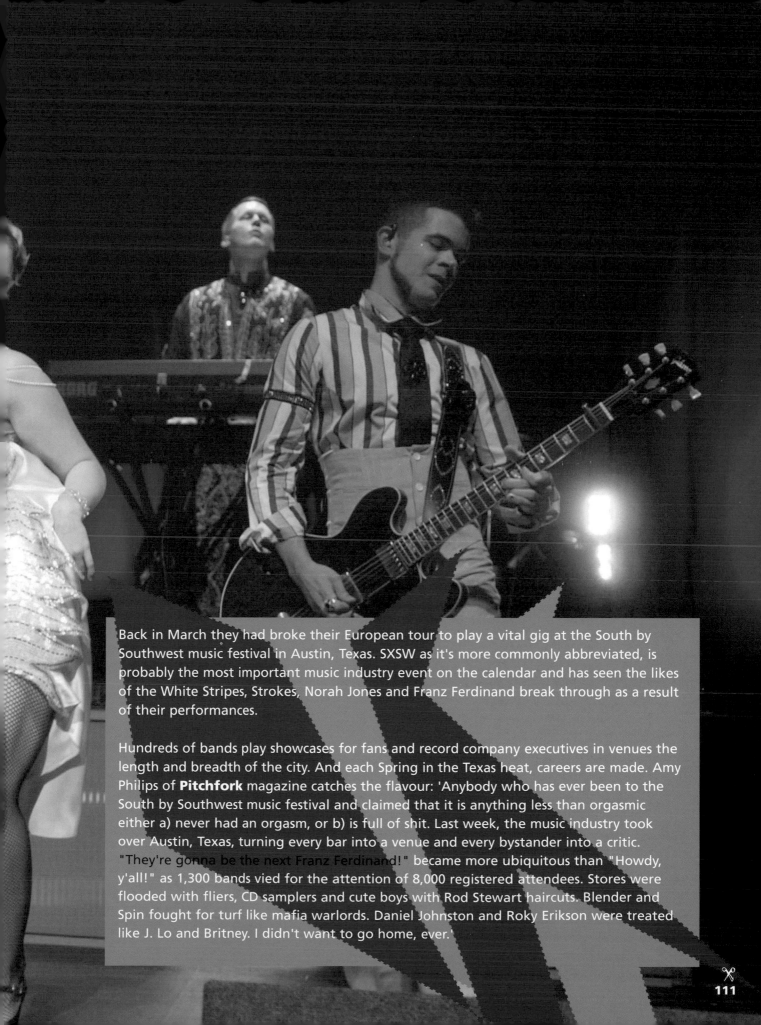

Back in March they had broke their European tour to play a vital gig at the South by Southwest music festival in Austin, Texas. SXSW as it's more commonly abbreviated, is probably the most important music industry event on the calendar and has seen the likes of the White Stripes, Strokes, Norah Jones and Franz Ferdinand break through as a result of their performances.

Hundreds of bands play showcases for fans and record company executives in venues the length and breadth of the city. And each Spring in the Texas heat, careers are made. Amy Philips of **Pitchfork** magazine catches the flavour: 'Anybody who has ever been to the South by Southwest music festival and claimed that it is anything less than orgasmic either a) never had an orgasm, or b) is full of shit. Last week, the music industry took over Austin, Texas, turning every bar into a venue and every bystander into a critic. "They're gonna be the next Franz Ferdinand!" became more ubiquitous than "Howdy, y'all!" as 1,300 bands vied for the attention of 8,000 registered attendees. Stores were flooded with fliers, CD samplers and cute boys with Rod Stewart haircuts. Blender and Spin fought for turf like mafia warlords. Daniel Johnston and Roky Erikson were treated like J. Lo and Britney. I didn't want to go home, ever.'

That March Scissor Sisters took to the stage with Junior Senior, a cross-over dance/indie two-piece from Denmark, and the B-52's, a Georgia band that had formed in the mid-1970s and who had made their name with singles such as 'Love Shack' in the late 1980s and the theme tune to Steven Spielberg's *Flintstones* feature film in 1993.

Bizarrely, SXSW has seen British bands signed to British labels, despite the crucial performances taking place in Texas. For Scissor Sisters – an American band signed to a UK label – it was a chance to ply their trade for the American music press.

The audiences were packed and happy, the press delighted but the head honchos in Universal were divided. Babydaddy analysed it, 'In the U.S, everything has to work within a certain niche. Either you're hard rock, hip-hop or new country. But so much of it is just knock-off band after knock-off band that you know it must be coming to an end. Something has to change.

'Anyway, why shouldn't we get played on the radio? We're making traditional pop music.'

It was tough. Again, college radio loved *Scissor Sisters*, as did the music press. But reaching the heartland – Middle America – was proving difficult. It was something that was going to take a good deal of time and patience.

Their debut album hit American record shop shelves in August and almost immediately, the band kicked off their promotional tour in Los Angeles. The **LA Times** decided that 'instead of campy flamboyance, the Scissor Sisters came on with pep-squad enthusiasm' and that Jake's 'bubbly good cheer was hard to resist.'

Time magazine called them '...the most enjoyable pop group to emerge in recent memory', largely because, it claimed, they understood the genre of pop so well. 'Pop music – where the same three chords have been swapping clothes for the past 50 years – is the nexus of the avant-garde and the conventional,' the journalist wrote, 'and on their debut, Shears, Babydaddy, Ana Matronic, Paddy Boom and Del Marquis walk the line with Madonna-like confidence.'

Back in the UK the media was keeping a beady eye on the proceedings. For the UK was, after all, where Scissor Sisters had first made their name. The **Daily Mirror**'s 3am Girls announced that the latest megastar to sign up to Scissor Sisters fan club was Bono. 'The singer popped backstage to see them after their gig at the PS1 gallery in Queens, New York, and told them how much he enjoyed their music,' they reported.

Earlier that evening Ana had stood on stage berating the American supermarket chain Wal-Mart for initially refusing to stock the Scissor Sisters album. Apparently the lyrics were deemed unsuitable for children, which Ana found ironic considering the shop sold guns and ammunition. By the volume of cheering it was a safe bet to conclude the audience was in complete agreement.

Ironically Wal-Mart evidently eventually decided to stock the album. On its website, a '*' replaced the 'i' in 'Tits on the Radio' but it told buyers the song 'is a snarling, swaggering attack on conservatism, recorded before the Janet Jackson/Superbowl wardrobe malfunction, but more relevant since that time.' Who writes Wal-Mart's copy? Will Self!

The gig that night in New York was an outdoor show and it had rained almost the entire length of the band's set. But it didn't stop the crowd from enjoying the show. Or Bono for that matter. Perhaps he had liked Ana's rant that – although didn't quite match his more political tirades – savaged what she had felt was hypocrisy on a grand scale. Afterwards, the Irish rock star headed backstage with his entourage and told Jake and his crew that they were the best pop band in the world.

At a late September concert in Washington DC a reporter from a local newspaper wrote: 'Scissor Sisters are already popular with the out-of-the-closet community... they play instantly catchy packages that are hard to resist no matter whom you date they are also dynamite musicians, able to seamlessly re-create the multilayered gloss of their album in a live setting.' In Atlanta they performed at the 99X Upstart Fest and another reviewer said Jake had a voice like Elton John and that he 'shimmers like a spit-shined disco ball retrieved from a crumbling '70s nightclub'. It was a compliment... of sorts.

Despite the difficulty in reaching mainstream America, the record industry at least was paying attention. 'Comfortably Numb' was nominated for a Grammy Award for Best Dance Recording. It was up against stiff competition. 'Good Luck' by Basement Jaxx, 'Get Yourself High' from The Chemical Brothers, 'Slow' by Kylie Minogue, and Britney Spears's 'Toxic' were all contenders for the coveted gong. It was going to be a tough contest. In the end – perhaps unsurprisingly – the Grammy went to Britney Spears. But just to be nominated was an achievement in itself.

Shortly afterwards though, Scissor Sisters would play a show that would mark the highlight of their career so far – at London's legendary Royal Albert Hall. The red brick and terracotta palace to the arts first opened in 1871 and was named after Prince Albert who died ten years before its completion. Since then the building has showcased the musical talents of all the great classical and rock giants.

In roughly twelve months Scissor Sisters had gone from entertaining 50 people at New York's gay clubs to headlining to 5,000 at one of the world's great musical venues.

Ana went straight up to the microphone after they had walked on stage. **'Is the Queen here?'** she asked. Dee Foran had gone to town on the outfits for this performance. Ana wore a silver flapper dress, in honour of her grandmother, and Jake was bare-chested (by now his trademark), under a gold waistcoat. 'At last, here are real pop stars who appear to have beamed down from a planet far more glamorous than our own, rather than emerging like production-line dummies in outfits that might have been thrown together by any bored stylist,' reported **Guardian**'s David Peschek.

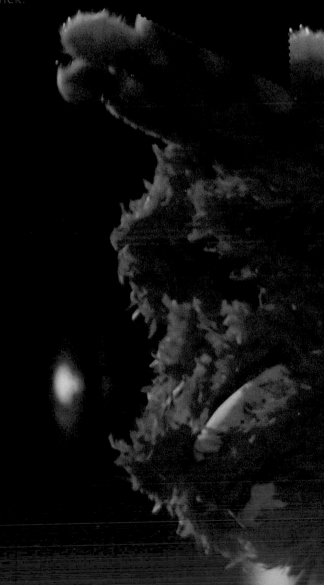

He continued in the same adulatory vein: 'Scissor Sisters were once best known for covering Pink Floyd's "Comfortably Numb" in the style of the Bee Gees, an idea even more daring and blasphemous than the Pet Shop Boys' appropriation of U2's "Where the Streets Have No Name". Tonight, the song's unmistakable opening riff predictably provokes a near riot. A lesser band would have sunk without trace as one-hit wonders; Scissor Sisters had an arsenal to back up that first hit.'

Shortly afterwards, at a show in Edinburgh's Corn Exchange – in a line-up that included transvestite singer called Kiki – when Scissor Sisters finally took to the stage Jake whipped off his waistcoat to reveal a catsuit with holes cut out for his nipples. It was Jake at his most fag-tastic but by now this kind of showmanship was expected.

The **Scotsman** heralded the no mean achievement of being able to draw the whoops and cheers from 'so many testosterone-fired lads' in the audience.

'Scissor Sisters unite not just those who know them from daytime radio and CD:UK, but cool club kids, indie fans and – naturally – every gay man and woman in the land' it concluded.

As an encore the band was joined on stage by Kiki together with a parade of gigantic dancing scissors for the song 'Take Your Mama'. It was a fitting end to a typically outrageous gig.

In December 2004 the band headed to New York's trendy Garment district to film the video for their new single 'Filthy/Gorgeous'.

They were joined by 100 transvestites and outrageously-clad fans from the clubbing world. But after trouble broke out between one particularly tall transvestite and a member of the film crew (the tranny had allegedly climbed a parking metre and spat on the crew member who retaliated by smashing a chair over his head), the police were called.

One report said 'stilettos were thrown, faces were scratched and wigs were pulled off'. After police had clubbed a few of the more macho trannies, things calmed down and filming resumed.

Jake, Ana, Del, Paddy and Babydaddy had asked director John Cameron Mitchell, co-creator/director of cult hit *Hedwig and the Angry Inch* to make the video for 'Filthy/Gorgeous'.' Mitchell had even starred in his 2001 film, taking the lead role as Hedwig, a boy born in East Berlin who falls in love with an American G.I. before undergoing a sex-change operation in order to marry him.

After Mitchell called 'wrap' on the 'Filthy/Gorgeous' set, the band knew the video may never actually get an official release. In the film band members were spanked and could be seen in compromising poses, exposed to a large number of sex toys and bare bodies. The song too was a little risqué – the subject matter of which was transvestite prostitutes. The lyrics went:

'When you're walkin' down the street
And a man tries to get your business
And the people that you meet
Want to open you up like Christmas

It was over the top – even by Jake's standards.

Jake however, was confident. 'The video is amazing. I think 'Filthy Gorgeous' is going to be our biggest single over there' (in the UK).

By December the number of units sold of their debut album had climbed to over one and a half million in the UK alone, topping British piano-led band Keane. End of year sales figured showed *Scissor Sisters* on top with 1,594,259 copies sold; Keane's *Hopes and Fears* on 1,593,677, followed by Robbie Williams Greatest Hits on 1.53 million and Maroon 5's *Songs about Jane* on 1.49 million. Incredibly, in the U.S. the band had sold just 150,000 copies.

Jake and Babydaddy had become prolific songwriters and, after becoming friendly with Kylie Minogue, she asked them to write something for her next album.

'The lady is a crack-up, a lot of fun to be around,' Jake noted. They wrote two songs for her album and 'I Believe in You' reached number two in the British charts at the years end.

On New Year's Eve Jake, Babydaddy, Ana, Del and Paddy joined Blondie to entertain 100,000 Hogmanay revellers in Edinburgh – just ahead of the release of Filthy/Gorgeous. It was quite a privilege considering Blondie was widely considered one of the most important bands of the New Wave punk era of the late 1970s. The band had formed in 1974 by art student guitarist Chris Stein and ex-Max's Kansas City waitress, vocalist Debbie Harry. Very much a New York band, Blondie cut their teeth at the – now legendary – CBGB's and Max's Kansas City. And in 1977 their eponymous debut had received rave reviews.

In January 2005, **The Advocate**, the US-based national gay and lesbian news magazine, announced:

'Dry your eyes, Erasure, Village People, and Pansy Division fans, and fork over that crown. It's official: The biggest, gayest band in the world is Scissor Sisters.'

The article quoted Babydaddy: 'It all happened so fast... I can't believe that our album wasn't even out a year ago.' **The Advocate** continued: 'The band navigated a slippery slope on their ascent. On one hand, they insisted that sexuality be part of the pitch. But they were also determined to be marketed as a mainstream pop group.'

Around this time the **Washington Post** noted that...

'America has yet to succumb to the charms of this particular, decidedly peculiar musical fashionista gumbo.'

It didn't matter that Middle America was still playing hard to get as in January the band was nominated for three Brit Awards in the UK: Best International Group, Best International Breakthrough Act and Best International Album.

In February it was announced they would be headlining that summer's V Festival after wowing the crowds the previous August. Unfortunately one of their most famous supporters, Kylie Minogue had to cancel her headline slot at the Glastonbury Festival after announcing she had developed breast cancer. It was a blow for the band because they had become close friends with the Aussie popette.

Scissor Sisters opened the 2005 Brit Awards with their hit 'Take Your Mama'. Ana and Jake emerged from two huge golden eggs onstage while a giant rooster together with singing watermelons danced around them. Their fans expected nothing less and afterwards The Express newspaper claimed that although the awards were called the Brits, it was the Americans who stole the show.

Other nominees that night included Jamelia, Joss Stone and Gwen Stefani, but the cameras singled out celebrity chavs Denise Van Outen and Sharon Osbourne who had bravely exposed their décolletage to the chill of February outside Earls Court.

In the Best International Group category Scissor Sisters were up against Green Day who had just released possibly *the* album of their career in *American Idiot*; Maroon 5 who had gained a vast fanbase with their catchy debut single 'Harder to Breathe'; the inimitable OutKast; and rock legends U2. For Best International Breakthrough Act they were competing against Jet, Kanye West, Killers and Maroon 5 once more. Finally, in the Best International Album category it was a similar roll call to Best International Group: The Killers' album *Hot Fuss*, Maroon 5's *Songs about Jane*, OutKast's *Speakerboxxx/The Love Below* and U2's *How to Dismantle an Atomic Bomb*.

It was a tough competition to say the least. But, remarkably, Scissor Sisters walked away with awards in all three of the categories in which they were nominated. Dressed in an antique Native American suit, Jake strode confidently to the stage to accept

the awards. 'It looks great but it smells of fish,' he joked, looking at the gong, adding: 'We decided to sing with puppets from Jim Henson's Creature Shop because we wanted a cross between Saturday morning TV and an acid trip'.

Afterwards the ceremony he told TV cameras: 'I feel like we've been adopted by Britain now. It feels like home because we've spent so much time here and people just really seem to get what we're about.' Ana told one interviewer:

'If you told us a year ago we would be getting these awards today we would have called you crazy.'

Franz Ferdinand triumphed, too, picking up awards for Best British Group and Best British Rock Act. Joss Stone was named best British Female Solo Artist as well as Best British Urban Act, while Mike Skinner's The Streets won British Male Solo Artist.

After the Brit Awards the band headed back to New York for some much needed R&R, to write new songs and begin work on the highly-anticipated follow-up to their debut record. It was also announced that Ana had collaborated with British electro-indie band New Order on a song called 'Jetstream', scheduled for release in May. The single featured remixes by Jacques Lu Cont, founder of Zoot Woman – the band which Scissor Sisters had supported way back on their first UK tour.

Ana considered it a great honour to work with New Order; in addition to the critical acclaim and a fan base that seemed to be growing daily, Scissor Sisters were also courting considerable recognition from other artists – most of whom were at the top of their field.

In 1980, New Order had sprung from the ashes of Joy Division following the suicide of singer Ian Curtis. Guitarist Bernard Sumner had taken on vocal duties and continued under the new name with bassist Peter Hook and percussionist / keyboard player Stephen Morris. In 2002, **Q** magazine listed New Order as was one of '50 Bands To See Before You Die'. It was no wonder Ana felt so flattered to be asked.

On March 3rd, Scissor Sisters announced through their website their support for Make Poverty History – the collective of charitable organisations whose aim it was to help stamp out world poverty and draw attention to the unfair global trade system. The gap between the worlds's rich and poor has never been wider, the collection claimed. 'Every single day, 30,000 children are dying as a result of extreme poverty. Malnutrition, AIDS, conflict and illiteracy are a daily reality for millions.' It was, they pointed out, '...due to man-made factors that the world was in such a state, and that poverty on such a scale didn't have to exist.

'OK, this is a music site, but sometimes you can't just sit back and do nothing,' the Scissor Sisters' website announced. The band was supporting the effort by the Make Poverty History collective 'in an effort to eradicate third world debt, aids and starvation'. Jake and the gang included links so that fans could email their MP or congressman and encouraged everyone to buy a white wristband or make a donation.

It was, perhaps, no surprise when the band announced it was honoured to have been asked to take part in the Live 8 show in London's Hyde Park in July, organised by Bob Geldof to encourage leaders of the G8 nations to eradicate third world debt. The line-up included U2, Elton, Paul McCartney, Madonna...

'Unlike Live Aid 20 years ago, he doesn't want people's money – he wants their voice,' the Live 8 website proclaimed. Attendance at the concert was free and would come a few days before the G8 leaders met in Edinburgh. Three billion people were to watch the concerts that took place take place in London, Paris, Berlin, Rome and Philadelphia. Meanwhile, thousands converged on Edinburgh to protest, during the summit, at the continuation and tolerance at what one commentator called 'this slow-motion holocaust'.

The band urged fans to peacefully march on Edinburgh, write to elected representatives and attend the concert. Once again, they included links to further information. Scissor Sisters were not merely signing up for good works but, like Geldorf, McCartney, Bono, Martin and the rest, actively promoting the cause.

Bob Geldof said the concerts were just one way in which all their voices could be heard in unison. 'This is without doubt,' he claimed, 'a moment in history where ordinary people can grasp the chance to achieve something truly monumental and demand from the eight world leaders at G8 an end to poverty.'

Live 8 was both a TV spectacular and, unlike Band Aid 20 years before, a political triumph. The G8 agreement a week later produced far more for aid, debt relief and commitments on reducing trade protectionism than it would have if Live 8 had not taken place.

At 8.15 pm on July 2 2005, Scissor Sisters came after a lacklustre Joss Stone and launched into 'Laura' – the crowd in Hyde Park went glam-ballistic. However serious the cause, it was time for the band to do what they do best –

entertain.

They followed it with 'Take your Mama', ending with 'Everyone wants the same thing'. It was a performance that was up with the best on the day.

The band was also doing their bit for AIDS awareness. Designers Against AIDS (DAA) was a fashion project launched to get AIDS back into the media. It manufactured T-shirts and tops by famous designers, DJs, musicians, photographers and sports stars. Scissor Sisters, The Cardigans and Robert Smith were among the recording artists to offer up some designs for the project. A portion of sales went to AIDS research.

As Jake sat in the bakery underneath his apartment back in 1999 he couldn't have dreamed of the scale of success he would achieve within the space of just six years.

There were no tell-tale signs of the million-plus albums they would shift, of their celebrity fans, or of the awards. It was all a dream in the mind of a man who would eventually take on the music world with his camp, but incendiary live show and incredible songwriting.

And make the dream real.